Tail of a Kite

COVER
ILLUSTRATOR

SPOTLIGHT

LILY TOY HONG

◆ "I've always wanted to be an artist as long as I can remember," says Lily Toy Hong. She was encouraged in her dream of illustrating children's books when her pictures won honors in a contest.

◆ Lily Toy Hong advises young artists to have fun. "Don't be afraid to try things," she says. She adds, "Look at colors, shapes—see things around you." This is just what Lily Toy Hong has done to create the lively shapes and colors of the cover's kites.

Acknowledgments appear on page 160, which constitutes an extension of this copyright page.

© 1993 Silver Burdett Ginn Inc.
Cover art © 1993 by Lily Toy Hong.

ISBN 0–663–54653–2

New Dimensions
IN THE
WORLD OF READING

Tail of a Kite

P R O G R A M   A U T H O R S

James F. Baumann   Roselmina Indrisano   P. David Pearson
Theodore Clymer   Dale D. Johnson   Taffy E. Raphael
Carl Grant   Connie Juel   Marian Davies Toth
Elfrieda H. Hiebert Jeanne R. Paratore   Richard L. Venezky

SILVER BURDETT GINN

NEEDHAM, MA   MORRISTOWN, NJ

ATLANTA, GA   DALLAS, TX   DEERFIELD, IL   MENLO PARK, CA

Unit 1 Theme

A Friend is a Friend

4

5

A Friend is a Friend

A friend can be a lot of help or just a lot of fun.

What's nice about having a friend?

THE FOURTH OF JULY, *wool, cotton, and nylon fabrics hooked on a burlap ground, 37 1/2" x 45 1/2". American, ca. 1940.*
Gift of Mr. Fred MacMurray. Courtesy of the Shelburne Museum, Shelburne, Vermont

Theme Books for
A Friend Is a Friend

*W**hy are friends so much fun? Are best friends always alike?**

✳ In **Chester's Way** by Kevin Henkes, Chester and Wilson are two mice friends who do *everything* together. Then Lilly moves into the neighborhood. They don't think they want Lilly for a friend. But Lilly has other ideas!

✽ Do you have a friend who always seems to be in trouble? Then you will understand Juan's problem in **Esmeralda and the Pet Parade** by Cecile Schoberle. Esmeralda is up to her ears in trouble!

More Books to Enjoy

Best Friends by Miriam Cohen

Amigo by Byrd Baylor

The White Marble by Charlotte Zolotow

Amelia Bedelia by Peggy Parish

Mitchell Is Moving

written by Marjorie Weinman Sharmat
illustrated by Jose Aruego & Ariane Dewey

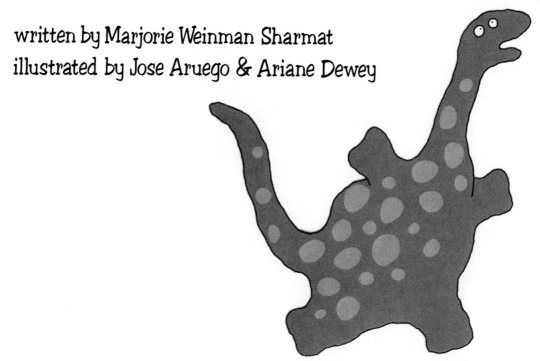

Mitchell ran through his house.

"So long. So long, everything," he shouted.

Then he ran next door to Margo's house.

"I'm moving," he said.

"Where?" asked Margo.

"Two weeks away," said Mitchell.

"Where is that?" asked Margo.

"It's wherever I will be after I walk for two weeks," said Mitchell. "I have lived in the same place for a long time. It is time for me to go someplace else."

"No!" said Margo. "You have only lived next door for fifty years."

"Sixty," said Mitchell.

"Fifty, sixty. What's the difference?" said Margo. "I want you to stay next door forever."

"I can't," said Mitchell. "I do not want to wake up in the same old bedroom and eat breakfast in the same old kitchen and brush my scales and clean my nails in the same old bathroom. Every room in my house is the same old room because I have been there too long."

"Well, maybe you are just tired of the same old friend," said Margo.

"Who is that?" asked Mitchell.

"Me," said Margo. "Maybe you look at me and think,

'Same Old Face.

Same Old Tail.

Same Old Scales.

Same Old Walk.

Same Old Talk.

Same Old Margo.'"

"No," said Mitchell. "I like your face, tail, scales, walk and talk. I like you."

"I like, like, like you," said Margo.

"I like, like, like you, too," said Mitchell.

He walked to the door. "I must pack," he said.

Margo sat down in front of the door. "You can't get out," she said. "I will sit here for another sixty years."

"I still like you!" shouted Mitchell as he climbed out the window.

Margo called after him, "I will glue you to your roof. I will tie you to your front door with a thick green rope. I will scotch-tape you, paper-clip you to your house. Then I will get a gigantic rubber band and loop you to your house. I will not let you leave."

14

15

"I will unglue, untie, untape, unclip and unloop myself," said Mitchell.

Mitchell ran around his house. "I'm moving, moving, moving," he shouted.

Then he gathered up some of the slimy moss near his house and wrapped it in silver foil. "Just in case there is no slimy moss two weeks away." Mitchell scooped up some mud from a ditch. "Maybe there is no mud two weeks away. Or no swamp water," he said as he filled a plastic bag with water from his swamp and mud from his ditch.

Mitchell went into his house and put the slimy moss and mud and swamp water into his suitcase.

The telephone rang. Mitchell answered it. "I will cement you to your ceiling," said Margo, and she hung up.

"I am beginning to think that Margo does not want me to move," said Mitchell as he went back to his packing. He packed the cap and mitten set that Margo had given him. "Maybe it will be cold two weeks away," he thought.

Mitchell heard a shout. He went to his window. Margo was shouting, "I will take you to the laundromat in my laundry bag, and I will wash away your idea of moving."

"Margo is a good shouter," thought Mitchell. He remembered when Margo had sent him a Happy Birthday Shout through the window:

"I'M GLAD YOU'RE THERE.

I'M GLAD I'M HERE.

HAPPY BIRTHDAY,

LOUD AND CLEAR."

"I wonder if there are any Happy Birthday Shouters two weeks away," thought Mitchell.

Mitchell held up the T-shirt that Margo had given him. It said,

MITCHELL, FRIEND OF MARGO

MARGO, FRIEND OF MITCHELL

"This shirt makes me feel sad that I am moving," said Mitchell. "But if I put it on I won't have to look at it." Mitchell put on the T-shirt. "If I don't look down at my chest, I will feel all right."

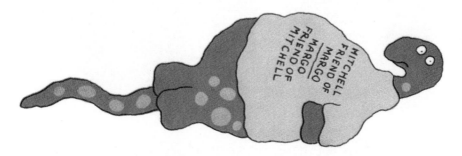

He closed his suitcase. "There. I am all packed. I am ready to go."

Mitchell walked through his house. "So long, same old rooms," he said.

Mitchell took his suitcase and went to Margo's house. "I am all ready to move," he said.

"I will stick you to your house with chewing gum," said Margo.

Mitchell picked up his suitcase and ran.

"Good-by!" he called. "I will write to you every day."

Mitchell stopped running and started to walk fast. "I am a moving Mitchell," he said.

Mitchell walked and walked.

When night came, he sent Margo a post card that said,

Dear Margo,

greetings from

one day away.

The second night he wrote,

Dear Margo,

more greetings from

two days away.

The third night he wrote,

Dear Margo,

more and more greetings

from three days away.

"I am not much of a post-card writer," thought Mitchell. But he sent more and more greetings to Margo each night.

At last Mitchell reached two weeks away. "I made it!" he said.

Mitchell built a house and moved in.

"I will go to bed right away so I can wake up in my new bedroom," he said.

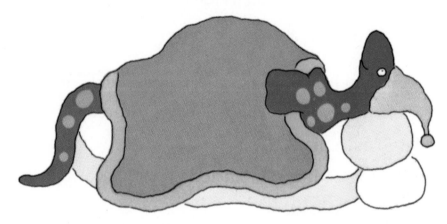

"Mmm. New sleeps better," Mitchell said the next day.

"Now I will eat my first meal in my new kitchen. Mmm. New tastes better."

Mitchell went outside and sat down in front of his house. "This is a good house," he said. "But there is something missing. There is nobody next door. What good is a good house when there is nobody next door to it? I am lonely. I miss Margo."

Mitchell wrote a post card to Margo:

Dear Margo,

the most greetings ever

from two weeks away.

The slimy moss is nice and slimy.

The mud is nice and thick.

The swamp water

is nice and mucky.

But I miss you.

Please come to see me.

Mitchell waited and waited. And waited.

One morning he woke up and saw a bottle of glue, a thick green rope, a big roll of Scotch tape, a huge paper clip, a gigantic rubber band, a laundry bag, a sack of cement and a package of chewing gum. Then he saw Margo.

"Mitchell!" said Margo.

"Margo!" said Mitchell. "I am so happy to see you. Here is my new house and my new everything." Mitchell showed Margo his new house and everything around it.

"Two weeks away is terrific," said Margo as she and Mitchell ate breakfast.

"No, it isn't," said Mitchell. "There is nobody next door."

"Oh," said Margo. "I have the same problem where I am. There is nobody next door."

"I have an idea," said Mitchell, and he got some twigs and mud.

"I have the same idea," said Margo, and she filled her laundry bag with more twigs and mud. Then she got her bottle of glue, thick green rope, big roll of Scotch tape, huge paper clip, gigantic rubber band and sack of cement.

"We can use these, too," she said.

Mitchell and Margo built a house next door to Mitchell's house.

"Do you like it?" asked Mitchell.

"It's perfect," said Margo. Margo moved into her new house.

She shouted,
"I'VE COME TO STAY
TWO WEEKS AWAY.
HAPPY BIRTHDAY."

It wasn't Mitchell's birthday.
But he was happy anyway.

Reader's Response ～ How would you
feel about moving away from a friend?

Mitchell's World

In the story, Mitchell moves two weeks away. How far do you think Mitchell the dinosaur could have traveled in two weeks?

In the time of the dinosaurs, the land of our planet may have looked very different. Some scientists think the world looked like this map.

You can see that the land was not separated by large oceans. Instead it was joined into one huge continent, which the scientists call Pangaea. That means that Mitchell could have walked from the United States to Africa without getting his feet wet!

According to the scientists, that would have been about 200 million years ago. In the time between then and now the continents have moved apart, and they still are moving! What do you think the world will look like in another 200 million years?

Gloria

WHO MIGHT BE MY BEST FRIEND

from **The Stories Julian Tells**

by Ann Cameron

If you have a girl for a friend, people find out and tease you. That's why I didn't want a girl for a friend—not until this summer, when I met Gloria.

It happened one afternoon when I was walking down the street by myself. My mother was visiting a friend of hers, and Huey was visiting a friend of his. Huey's friend is five and so I think he is too young to play with. And there aren't any kids just my age. I was walking down the street feeling lonely.

A block from our house I saw a moving van in front of a brown house, and men were carrying in chairs and tables and bookcases and boxes full of I don't know what. I watched for a while, and suddenly I heard a voice right behind me.

"Who are you?"

I turned around and there was a girl in a yellow dress. She looked the same age as me. She had curly hair that was braided into two pigtails with red ribbons at the ends.

"I'm Julian," I said. "Who are you?"

"I'm Gloria," she said. "I come from Newport. Do you know where Newport is?"

I wasn't sure, but I didn't tell Gloria. "It's a town on the ocean," I said.

"Right," Gloria said. "Can you turn a cartwheel?"

She turned sideways herself and did two cartwheels on the grass.

I had never tried a cartwheel before, but I tried to copy Gloria. My hands went down in the grass, my feet went up in the air, and—I fell over.

I looked at Gloria to see if she was laughing at me. If she was laughing at me, I was going to go home and forget about her.

But she just looked at me very seriously and said, "It takes practice," and then I liked her.

"I know where there's a bird's nest in your yard," I said.

"Really?" Gloria said. "There weren't any trees in the yard, or any birds, where I lived before."

I showed her where a robin lives and has eggs. Gloria stood up on a branch and looked in. The eggs were small and pale blue. The mother robin squawked at us, and she and the father robin flew around our heads.

"They want us to go away," Gloria said. She got down from the branch, and we went around to the front of the house and watched the moving men carry two rugs and a mirror inside.

"Would you like to come over to my house?" I said.

"All right," Gloria said, "if it is all right with my mother." She ran in the house and asked.

It was all right, so Gloria and I went to my house, and I showed her my room and my games and my rock collection, and then I made strawberry Kool-Aid and we sat at the kitchen table and drank it.

"You have a red mustache on your mouth," Gloria said.

"You have a red mustache on your mouth, too," I said.

Gloria giggled, and we licked off the mustaches with our tongues.

"I wish you'd live here a long time," I told Gloria.

Gloria said, "I wish I would too.

"I know the best way to make wishes," Gloria said.

"What's that?" I asked.

"First you make a kite. Do you know how to make one?"

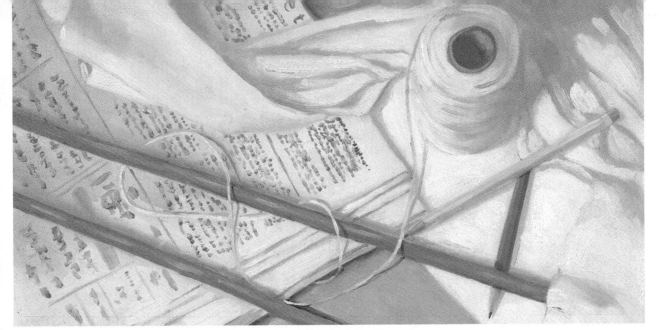

"Yes," I said, "I know how." I know how to make good kites because my father taught me. We make them out of two crossed sticks and folded newspaper.

"All right," Gloria said, "that's the first part of making wishes that come true. So let's make a kite."

We went out into the garage and spread out sticks and newspaper and made a kite. I fastened on the kite string and went to the closet and got rags for the tail.

"Do you have some paper and two pencils?" Gloria asked. "Because now we make the wishes."

I didn't know what she was planning, but I went in the house and got pencils and paper.

"All right," Gloria said. "Every wish you want to have come true you write on a long thin piece of paper. You don't tell me your wishes, and I don't tell you mine. If you tell, your wishes don't come true. Also, if you look at the other person's wishes, your wishes don't come true."

Gloria sat down on the garage floor again and started writing her wishes. I wanted to see what they were—but I went to the other side of the garage and wrote my own wishes instead. I wrote:

1. I wish I could see the catalog cats.

2. I wish the fig tree would be the tallest in town.

3. I wish I'd be a great soccer player.

4. I wish I could ride in an airplane.

5. I wish Gloria would stay here and be my best friend.

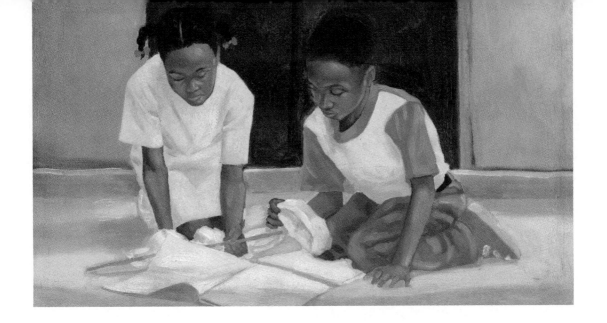

I folded my five wishes in my fist and went over to Gloria.

"How many wishes did you make?" Gloria asked.

"Five," I said. "How many did you make?"

"Two," Gloria said.

I wondered what they were.

"Now we put the wishes on the tail of the kite," Gloria said. "Every time we tie one piece of rag on the tail, we fasten a wish in the knot. You can put yours in first."

I fastened mine in, and then Gloria fastened in hers, and we carried the kite into the yard.

"You hold the tail," I told Gloria, "and I'll pull."

We ran through the back yard with the kite, passed the garden and the fig tree, and went into the open field beyond our yard.

The kite started to rise. The tail jerked heavily like a long white snake. In a minute the kite passed the roof of my house and was climbing toward the sun.

We stood in the open field, looking up at it. I was wishing I would get my wishes.

"I know it's going to work!" Gloria said.

"How do you know?"

"When we take the kite down," Gloria told me, "there shouldn't be one wish in the tail. When the wind takes all your wishes, that's when you know it's going to work."

The kite stayed up for a long time. We both held the string. The kite looked like a tiny black spot in the sun, and my neck got stiff from looking at it.

"Shall we pull it in?" I asked.

"All right," Gloria said.

We drew the string in more and more until, like a tired bird, the kite fell at our feet.

We looked at the tail. All our wishes were gone. Probably they were still flying higher and higher in the wind.

Maybe I would see the catalog cats and get to be a good soccer player and have a ride in an airplane and the tallest fig tree in town. And Gloria would be my best friend.

"Gloria," I said, "did you wish we would be friends?"

"You're not supposed to ask me that!" Gloria said.

"I'm sorry," I answered. But inside I was smiling. I guessed one thing Gloria wished for. I was pretty sure we would be friends.

Reader's Response ∼ Will Julian and Gloria become good friends? Tell why or why not.

Library Link ∼ *You can read about the invisible catalog cats and Julian's fig tree in* The Stories Julian Tells.

Kites

Today we fly kites for fun. But people have also used kites for science, for sending messages, and for celebrating holidays.

The first kites probably were made about 3,000 years ago in Asia. Some of the oldest kites were made from large leaves and flown with vines instead of string.

People used to think kites had a special power. Flying them was like climbing toward heaven. Long ago in China, people flew kites to bring them good luck and happiness. No wonder Gloria attached wishes to her kite!

How does seeing a kite soar through the sky make you feel? How would it feel to be able to fly like a kite?

Reply to Someone Who Asked Why the Two of Us Are Such Good Friends

by Beatrice Schenk de Regniers

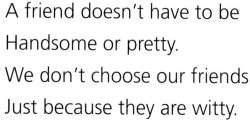

A friend doesn't have to be
Handsome or pretty.
We don't choose our friends
Just because they are witty.

My friend isn't perfect.
Others may be
Smarter or sweeter
Or nicer to me.

And sometimes we fight,
But that's quite all right —
—If we're mad in the morning,
We make up before night —
Because
    a friend
        is a friend
            is a friend.

Why are we friends?
Don't ask us why.
We can't explain.
We won't even try.

Friends are not perfect.
They've plenty of flaws.
But that doesn't matter at all
Because
      a friend
        is a friend
          is a friend.
    So…

Whoever we are,
Whatever we be,
We're friends 'cause I'm I,
We're friends 'cause she's she.
(Or because he is he —
Whatever, whatever the case may be.)
    A friend
       is a friend
          is a friend!

Aug. 5
Dear Susie,
p is fun. Today
I rode a horse.
I miss you.
Love,
Olivia

BE TRUE

POS

Susie,
250 Gr
San Fran
Californ

Tony's Hard Work Day

written by Alan Arkin
pictures by James Stevenson

One time Tony's mother and father bought a house in the country. It was a small house and very broken, but Tony's father liked it because there was green grass everywhere and sweet water and good air that you could breathe all day long.

"Smell the air!" Tony's father would say, and everyone would stop what they were doing and breathe in and out.

There was a lot of work to do in the country. Painting work and cleaning work and hanging up curtains and taking down spider webs and hammering and nailing and things like that.

"Let me help," Tony would say to his father. "Let me hammer."

"No, you are too small," Tony's father would answer. "You would hit yourself with the hammer, and then you would cry, and we would all have to stop working and hold you for a little while, so it's not a good idea."

"Let me help!" Tony said to his mother, who was sewing curtains.

"Not right now," said Tony's mother, "because I'm making tiny, tiny stitches with my needle, and your hands aren't smart enough to do such small work, and you would stick yourself and a little blood would come, and you hate blood, and then you would cry, and we would all have to stop working and rock you and sing to you, so that's not a good idea."

"Let me help," Tony said to his big brother Matthew, who was painting his room with a big brush.

"No," said Matthew, "you don't know how to paint, and you will make a mess on the floor and then I will get angry and yell at you, and you will cry and run to Mommy, and she will ask you what's wrong, and you will tell her that I was mean to you, and she will tell Daddy, and he will yell at me, so that's not a good idea."

"Let me help," Tony said to his other big brother Adam, who was chopping wood.

"No," said Adam, "this axe is very heavy and you won't be able to lift it very high, and it will drop fast and fall on your foot, and you will yell and jump around for ten minutes, so that's not a good idea."

"But what will be a good idea for me?" Tony asked his brother.

"A good idea for you is to go and play someplace where you don't bother anybody," said Adam.

"OK," said Tony, and he took a walk to where there was a big hill. "I will build my own house," he said.

So Tony dug a big hole in the ground. Then he filled up the hole with pebbles and stones, and smoothed it down carefully until it was flat.

"That will be the floor," said Tony.

Then Tony made an axe out of a sharp
rock and a stick.

"I will chop down some trees for the walls
of my house," he said.

And he chopped down a hundred trees and cut the tops so they turned into logs. Then he cut little pieces from the ends so they would fit together, and he rolled them over to the stone floor. Then he put one log on top of another to make the walls of his house.

But pretty soon the walls were so high that he couldn't reach the top, so he went home to get a ladder.

"Now I can reach the top," he said.

Tony finished putting up the walls of his house and then cut down a hundred more trees to make the roof.

He put one tree right next to another on top of the house, and when that was done he went into the woods and got some vines.

He pulled the leaves from the vines until he had a long rope and then he tied all the trees on the roof together.

Then he made some mud with water and dirt and smeared it all over the roof so the rain wouldn't get in.

Then he chopped big square holes in the walls with his axe.

"Those will be my windows," said Tony.

When he was done with the windows he went home for lunch. He was very hungry from all that work, so he ate five sandwiches and drank seven glasses of milk.

"What have you been doing all morning?" said Tony's father.

"Playing a game on the hill," said Tony and he went back to work.

He got a thousand rocks and piled them
up on top of each other inside the house, and
when he came to the ceiling he cut a hole so a
chimney could go through.

"This will be my fireplace," said Tony.

Then he put mud between all the rocks so
the fireplace would stay up forever.

Then he got some of the tall, tall grass that grew in the meadow and he wove a big rug for his house, so his feet would be warm when his shoes were off.

Then he took a nap because he was all tired out from his hard work.

When he woke up, the whole family was standing over him.

"We couldn't find you anywhere," said his mother.

"I was sleeping," said Tony.

"Who made this beautiful house?" asked Tony's father.

"I did," said Tony, "and it was very hard work. It took me the whole day."

"It looks like a good place to live," said Adam.

"Can we stay in this house with you?" asked Matthew.

"Sure," said Tony.

So they moved all the beds and dishes into the house Tony built. And they were so happy there that they stayed in the country forever, and whenever there was any work to do they would say to Tony, "Can I help?"

And Tony would always say, "Yes."

Reader's Response ∾ What would you say to Tony if he wanted to help you?

Busy As a Bee

Could you build a house in one day like Tony? You certainly couldn't do it all by yourself. But what if you had help?

In pioneer days, men worked together to build a barn. They called it a "raising bee" or a "barn raising."

Women had "quilting bees," and everyone liked "husking bees," racing to see who could husk corn the fastest. After the work was finished, the families ate and sometimes danced. A "bee" was a great way to do a big job and have a party at the same time.

What job could your class do together? How could you work and have fun, too?

A Special Trade

written by Sally Wittman
illustrated by Karen Gundersheimer

Old Bartholomew is Nelly's neighbor.
When Nelly was very small, he would take
her every day for a walk down the block to
Mrs. Pringle's vegetable garden.

Bartholomew never pushed too fast.
He always warned Nelly about Mr. Oliver's
bumpy driveway:

"Hang on, Nell! Here's a bump!"

And she'd shout "BUMP!" as she rode over it.

If they met a nice dog along the way, they'd stop and pet it. But if it was nasty, Bartholomew would shoo it away.

When Mrs. Pringle's sprinkler was on, he would say, "Get ready, get set, CHAAARRRRRRRRRRRRGE!"

Nelly would squeal "Wheeeee!" as he pushed her through it.

57

When Nelly began to walk, Bartholomew took her by the hand. "NO-NO!" she cried, pulling it back. Nelly didn't want any help. So Bartholomew offered his hand only when she really needed it.

Bartholomew was getting older, too. He needed a walking stick. So they walked very slowly. When they walked upstairs, they *both* held on to the railing.

The neighbors called them "ham and eggs" because they were always together.

Even on Halloween. And on the coldest day of winter when everyone else was inside.

One summer Bartholomew taught Nelly to skate by circling his walking stick. "Easy does it!" he warned. Then she skated right over his toes! He wasn't mad, though. He just whistled and rubbed his foot.

The first time Nelly tried to skate by herself she fell. Bartholomew saw that she felt like crying. He pulled up something from the garden and said, "Don't be saddish, have a radish!"

Nelly laughed and ate it. She didn't really like radishes, but she did like Bartholomew.

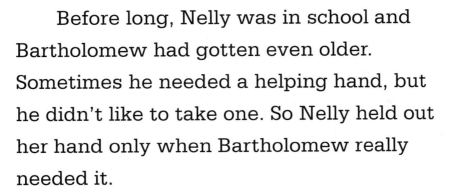

Before long, Nelly was in school and Bartholomew had gotten even older. Sometimes he needed a helping hand, but he didn't like to take one. So Nelly held out her hand only when Bartholomew really needed it.

Whenever Bartholomew had to stop and rest, Nelly would beg for a story about the "old days." Once after a story, she asked him, "Will we ever run out of things to talk about?"

"If we do," said Bartholomew, "we just won't say anything. Good friends can do that."

Some days they just took it easy and sat on the porch. Bartholomew would play a tune on his harmonica. Nelly would make up the words.

One day Bartholomew went out alone and fell down the stairs. An ambulance with a red flasher and a siren took him to the hospital. He was gone for a long time.

Nelly wrote him every day. She always ended with, "Come back soon, so we can go for walks again."

When Bartholomew came home, he was in a wheelchair. The smile was gone from his eyes.

"I guess our walks are over," he said.

"No they aren't," said Nelly.

"*I* can take *you* for walks now."

She knew just how to do it, too. Nice and easy, not too fast. Just before Mr. Oliver's driveway, she would call, "Get ready for the bump!"

And Bartholomew would wave his hat like a cowboy as he rode over it.

If they saw a nice dog, they'd stop and pet it. But if it was mean, Nelly would shoo it away.

One day when the sprinkler was on, Nelly started to go around. But she changed her mind. "All right, Bartholomew. Ready, set, one, two, three. CHAAARRRRRRRRRRRRGE!" And she pushed him right through it!

"Ah...that was fun!" said Bartholomew.

Nelly grinned. "I hope your wheelchair won't rust."

"Fiddlesticks!" He laughed. "Who cares if it does!"

Mrs. Pringle leaned over the fence. "Seems just like yesterday Bartholomew was pushing *you* in the stroller."

"That was when I was little," said Nelly. "Now it's my turn to push and Bartholomew's turn to sit...kind of like a trade."

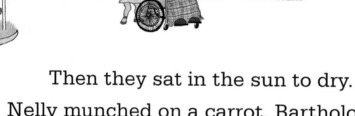

Then they sat in the sun to dry. Nelly munched on a carrot. Bartholomew played a tune on his harmonica. Nelly could see the old smile was back in Bartholomew's eyes.

Reader's Response 〜 Nelly liked to take Bartholomew for a ride. How can you help the grown-ups you know?

A Special Storyteller

Do you think Nelly and Bartholomew, the "ham and eggs" friends, ever heard the story about green eggs and ham? Have you? Or do you know the Grinch or the Cat in the Hat? You do if you've read books by Dr. Seuss (rhymes with "goose").

Dr. Seuss began writing his first book for children on a trip across the ocean. He listened to the ship's engine and wrote the words to its beat. The book was *And to Think That I Saw It on Mulberry Street.* Can you hear the beat as you say the title?

Throughout his life, Dr. Seuss made reading fun for children like Nelly. But when he was 82, he came out with *You're Only Old Once,* a special book for people who are growing older, just like Bartholomew.

Tikki Tikki Tembo

retold by Arlene Mosel
illustrated by Blair Lent

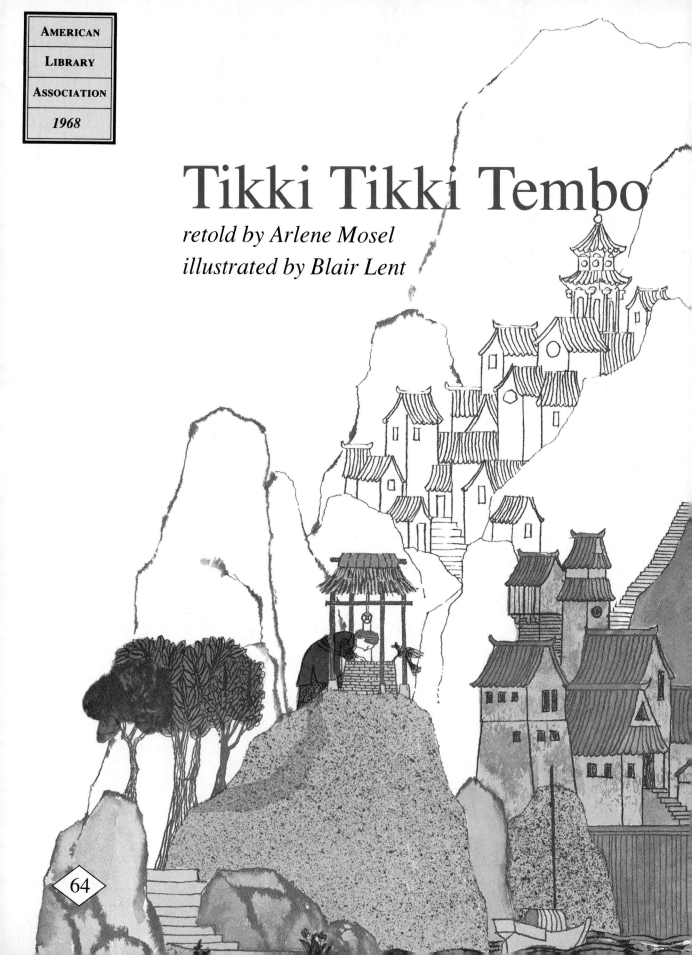

Once upon a time, a long, long time ago,
it was the custom of all the fathers and mothers
in China to give their first and honored sons great
long names. But second sons were given hardly
any name at all.

In a small mountain village there lived a
mother who had two little sons. Her second son
she called Chang, which meant "little or
nothing." But her first and honored son, she
called Tikki tikki tembo-no sa rembo-chari bari
ruchi-pip peri pembo, which meant "the most
wonderful thing in the whole wide world!"

Every morning the mother went to wash in a little stream near her home. The two boys always went chattering along with her. On the bank was an old well.

"Don't go near the well," warned the mother, "or you will surely fall in."

The boys did not always mind their mother
and one day they were playing beside the well,
and on the well when Chang fell in!

Tikki tikki tembo-no sa rembo-chari bari ruchi-pip peri pembo ran as fast as his little legs could carry him to his mother and said,

"Most Honorable Mother, Chang has fallen into the well!"

"The water roars, 'Little Blossom,' I cannot hear you," said the mother.

Then Tikki tikki tembo-no sa rembo-chari bari ruchi-pip peri pembo raised his voice and cried,

"Oh, Most Honorable One, Chang has fallen into the well!"

"That troublesome boy," answered the mother. "Run and get the Old Man With The Ladder to fish him out."

Then Tikki tikki tembo-no sa rembo-chari bari ruchi-pip peri pembo ran as fast as his little legs could carry him to the Old Man With The Ladder and said,

"Old Man With The Ladder, Chang has fallen into the well. Will you come and fish him out?"

"So," said the Old Man With The Ladder, "Chang has fallen into the well."

And he ran as fast as his old legs could carry him. Step over step, step over step he went into the well, picked up little Chang, and step over step, step over step brought him out of the well.

He pumped the water out of him and pushed the air into him, and pumped the water out of him and pushed the air into him, and soon Chang was just as good as ever!

Now for several months the boys did not go near the well. But after the Festival of the Eighth Moon they ran to the well to eat their rice cakes.

They ate near the well, they played around the well, they walked on the well and Tikki tikki tembo-no sa rembo-chari bari ruchi-pip peri pembo fell into the well!

Chang ran as fast as his little legs could carry him to his mother and said,

"Oh, Most Honorable Mother, Tikki tikki tembo-no sa rembo-chari bari ruchi-pip peri pembo has fallen into the well!"

"The water roars, 'Little One,' I cannot hear you."

So little Chang took a deep breath.

"Oh, Mother, Most Honorable," he panted, "Tikki tikki tembo-no sa rembo-chari bari ruchi-pip peri pembo has fallen into the well!"

"Tiresome Child, what are you trying to say?" said his mother.

"Honorable Mother! Chari bari rembo tikki tikki," he gasped, "pip pip has fallen into the well!"

"Unfortunate Son, surely the evil spirits have bewitched your tongue. Speak your brother's name with reverence."

Poor little Chang was all out of breath from saying that great long name, and he didn't think he could say it one more time. But then he thought of his brother in the old well.

Chang bowed his little head clear to the sand, took a deep breath and slowly, very slowly said,

"Most Honorable Mother, Tikki tikki—tembo-no—sa rembo—chari bari—ruchi-pip—peri pembo is at the bottom of the well."

"Oh, not my first and honored son, heir of all I possess! Run quickly and tell the Old Man With The Ladder that your brother has fallen into the well."

So Chang ran as fast as his little legs would carry him to the Old Man With The Ladder. Under a tree the Old Man With The Ladder sat bowed and silent.

"Old Man, Old Man," shouted Chang. "Come right away! Tikki tikki tembo-no sa rembo-chari bari ruchi-pip peri pembo has fallen into the stone well!"

But there was no answer. Puzzled he waited.
Then with his very last bit of breath he shouted,

"Old Man With The Ladder, Tikki tikki
tembo-no sa rembo-chari bari ruchi-pip peri
pembo is at the bottom of the well."

"Miserable child, you disturb my dream. I
had floated into a purple mist and found my
youth again. There were glittering gateways and
jeweled blossoms. If I close my eyes perhaps I will
again return."

Poor little Chang
was frightened.
How could he
say that great
long name again?

"Please, Old Man
With The Ladder,
please help my brother
out of the cold well."

"So," said the Old Man With The Ladder, "your mother's 'Precious Pearl' has fallen into the well!"

The Old Man With The Ladder hurried as fast as his old legs could carry him. Step over step, step over step he went into the well, and step over step, step over step out of the well with the little boy in his arms. Then he pumped the water out of him and pushed the air into him, and pumped the water out of him and pushed the air into him.

But little Tikki tikki tembo-no sa rembo-chari bari ruchi-pip peri pembo had been in the water so long, all because of his great long name, that the moon rose many times before he was quite the same again.

And from that day to this the Chinese have always thought it wise to give all their children little, short names instead of great long names.

Reader's Response ～ How do you think Tikki tikki tembo felt about having such a long name?

Animal Tales

Animals in stories do all kinds of things.

How can we tell what is real and what is make-believe?

CHESHIRE CAT IN CROUCHED POSITION, *illustration by Randolph Caldecott, British (1846-1886)*

Theme Books for
Animal Tales

*A*nimals are fun to watch and exciting to read about. When you pretend that they can talk and do amazing things, then almost anything can happen!

✳ *Sylvester and the Magic Pebble* by William Steig is about a young donkey who finds a pebble that makes his wishes come true. He thinks that all his troubles are over, but they are really just beginning!

Sylvester
and the
Magic Pebble

WILLIAM STEIG

※ What in the world is a wombat? And who has heard of a platypus or a dingo? All of these animals live in Australia. When you read *Wombat Stew* by Marcia K. Vaughan, you will discover how Dingo is tricked out of a meal.

More Books to Enjoy

Frog and Toad Are Friends by Arnold Lobel
George and Martha Back in Town by James Marshall
Four Stories for Four Seasons by Tomie dePaola
Winnie-the-Pooh by A. A. Milne

What A Clever Toad I Am!
from *The Wind in the Willows*

by Kenneth Grahame

The world has held great Heroes,
  As history-books have showed;
But never a name to go down to fame
  Compared with that of Toad!

The clever men at Oxford
  Know all that there is to be knowed.
But they none of them know one half as much
  As intelligent Mr. Toad!

Animal Fact/ ANIMAL FABLE

from the book by **Seymour Simon**
illustrated by Diane de Groat

Many of us like to watch animals. You may have a pet dog or cat. At times you may notice that your pet moves its tail differently when it's happy than when it's angry. After watching your pet for a long time, you can probably tell a great deal about what each kind of tail movement means.

But even if you watch animals closely, it is sometimes easy to mistake what is happening. For example, a bat flutters around in an odd way in the night sky. Some people may think that bats are blind and can't see where they are going.

If bats are really blind, that belief is true; it is a fact. But suppose the bat flies in that odd way for another reason, and is not really blind. Then the belief is a fable; it is not true.

Next we'll look at some common beliefs about animals. Guess if each belief is a fact or a fable; then turn the page to find the answer. You will also discover why scientists think the belief is a fact or a fable.

SOME FISH CAN CLIMB TREES

FACT Most fish can't climb trees, but the mud skipper can. Skippers climb up logs or the branches of trees that lean into the water. Even when out of the water, skippers can breathe air through their gills.

The mud skipper lives in many parts of the world. It looks like a mixture of a fish, a tadpole, and a frog. Skippers use their thick front fins to skip about on the land. They are looking for insects and other things to eat.

PORCUPINES SHOOT THEIR QUILLS

FABLE Porcupines cannot really shoot their quills. A porcupine's quills are sharp and have barbs like tiny hooks. The tip of a quill shown here has been magnified many times. When the quill sinks into an animal it becomes stuck and is left behind.

Porcupines use their quills to protect themselves. If an animal or person bothers a porcupine, the quills stand on end. The porcupine turns around and backs up to his enemy. Few animals bother a porcupine a second time.

DOGS TALK WITH THEIR TAILS

FACT We know dogs don't use words to talk, but their tails can tell us how they feel. When a dog wags its tail from side to side, the dog is happy and playful. But when a dog wags its tail up and down, it may be because it has done something wrong and expects to be punished.

If a dog keeps its tail straight up, be careful. That is the signal that it may attack. Don't run, just back away slowly.

OSTRICHES HIDE THEIR HEADS IN THE SAND

FABLE There is a well-known fable that ostriches stick their heads in the sand when they are frightened. Here's how the fable may have started. When ostriches see an enemy, they sometimes drop down and stretch out their necks along the ground. This makes it more difficult for the enemy to see them. To a person watching an ostrich, it may look as if the ostrich has buried its head in the ground.

An ostrich may not be very smart, but it is not dumb. When an enemy comes close, the ostrich gets up from the ground and runs away.

Reader's Response ⌒ Which animal fact or fable surprised you most? Tell why.

UP CLOSE!

How do people learn about animals? Scientists called zoologists watch them closely and write down what they find out.

Jane Goodall is a zoologist. She studies a kind of ape called the chimpanzee. She gets up early each morning and goes right into the African forest to follow chimpanzee families.

When Jane Goodall first started following them, the apes were very shy. But after a while, they let her get very close. Then one day a chimp even held her hand for a second. Since then, she has been able to watch them up close and tell us all about them.

Have you ever watched an animal very closely? What did you learn?

SNAIL

Little snail,
Dreaming you go.
Weather and rose
Is all you know.

Weather and rose
Is all you see,
Drinking
The dewdrop's
Mystery.

Langston Hughes

A Moment in Summer

A moment in summer
belongs to me
and one particular
honey bee.
A moment in summer
shimmering clear
making the sky
seem very near,
a moment in summer
belongs to me.

Charlotte Zolotow

The
Goat
in the Rug

as told to Charles L. Blood & Martin Link
illustrated by Nancy Winslow Parker

My name is Geraldine and I live near a place called Window Rock with my Navajo friend, Glenmae. It's called Window Rock because it has a big round hole in it that looks like a window open to the sky. Glenmae is called Glenmae most of the time because it's easier to say than her Indian name: Glee 'Nasbah. In English that means something like female warrior, but she's really a Navajo weaver. I guess that's why, one day, she decided to weave me into a rug.

I remember it was a warm, sunny afternoon. Glenmae had spent most of the morning sharpening a large pair of scissors. I had no idea what she was going to use them for, but it didn't take me long to find out.

Before I knew what was happening, I was on the ground and Glenmae was clipping off my wool in great long strands. (It's called mohair, really.) It didn't hurt at all, but I admit I kicked up my heels some. I'm very ticklish for a goat.

I might have looked a little naked and silly afterwards, but my, did I feel nice and cool! So I decided to stick around and see what would happen next.

The first thing Glenmae did was chop up roots from a yucca plant. The roots made a soapy, rich lather when she mixed them with water. She washed my wool in the suds until it was clean and white. After that, a little bit of me (you might say) was hung up in the sun to dry. When my wool was dry, Glenmae took out two large square combs with many teeth.

By combing my wool between these carding combs, as they're called, she removed any bits of twigs or burrs and straightened out the fibers. She told me it helped make a smoother yarn for spinning.

Then, Glenmae carefully started to spin my wool—one small bundle at a time—into yarn. I was beginning to find out it takes a long while to make a Navajo rug.

Again and again, Glenmae twisted and
pulled, twisted and pulled the wool. Then
she spun it around a long, thin stick she
called a spindle. As she twisted and pulled
and spun, the finer, stronger and smoother
the yarn became.

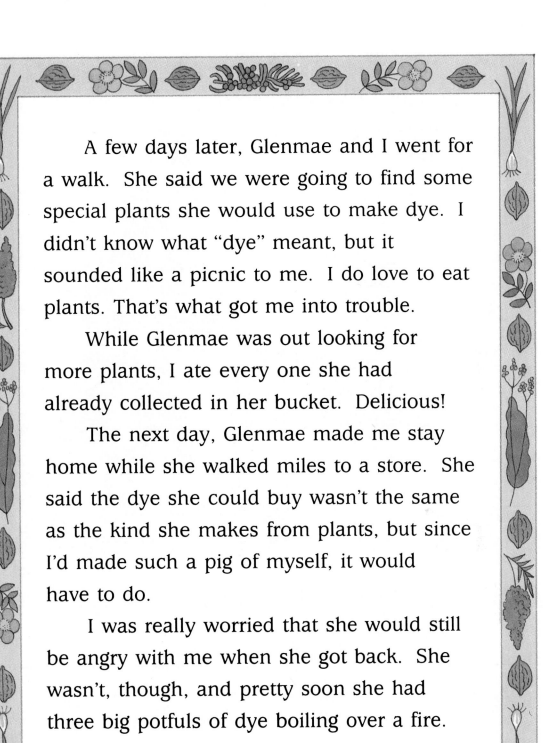

A few days later, Glenmae and I went for a walk. She said we were going to find some special plants she would use to make dye. I didn't know what "dye" meant, but it sounded like a picnic to me. I do love to eat plants. That's what got me into trouble.

While Glenmae was out looking for more plants, I ate every one she had already collected in her bucket. Delicious!

The next day, Glenmae made me stay home while she walked miles to a store. She said the dye she could buy wasn't the same as the kind she makes from plants, but since I'd made such a pig of myself, it would have to do.

I was really worried that she would still be angry with me when she got back. She wasn't, though, and pretty soon she had three big potfuls of dye boiling over a fire.

Then I saw what Glenmae had meant by
dyeing. She dipped my white wool into one
pot . . . and it turned pink! She dipped it in
again. It turned a darker pink! By the time
she'd finished dipping it in and out and hung
it up to dry, it was a beautiful deep red.

After that, she dyed some of my wool brown, and some of it black. I couldn't help wondering if those plants I'd eaten would turn all of me the same colors.

While I was worrying about that, Glenmae started to make our rug. She took a ball of yarn and wrapped it around and around two poles. I lost count when she'd reached three hundred wraps. I guess I was too busy thinking about what it would be like to be the only red, white, black and brown goat at Window Rock.

It wasn't long before Glenmae had finished wrapping. Then she hung the poles with the yarn on a big wooden frame. It looked like a picture frame made of logs— she called it a "loom."

After a whole week of getting ready to weave, Glenmae started. She began weaving at the bottom of the loom. Then, one strand of yarn at a time, our rug started growing toward the top. A few strands of black. A few of brown. A few of red. In and out. Back and forth. Until, in a few days, the pattern of our rug was clear to see.

Our rug grew very slowly. Just as every Navajo weaver before her had done for hundreds and hundreds of years, Glenmae formed a design that would never be duplicated.

Then, at last, the weaving was finished! But not until I'd checked it quite thoroughly in front . . . and in back, did I let Glenmae take our rug off the loom. There was a lot of me in that rug. I wanted it to be perfect. And it was.

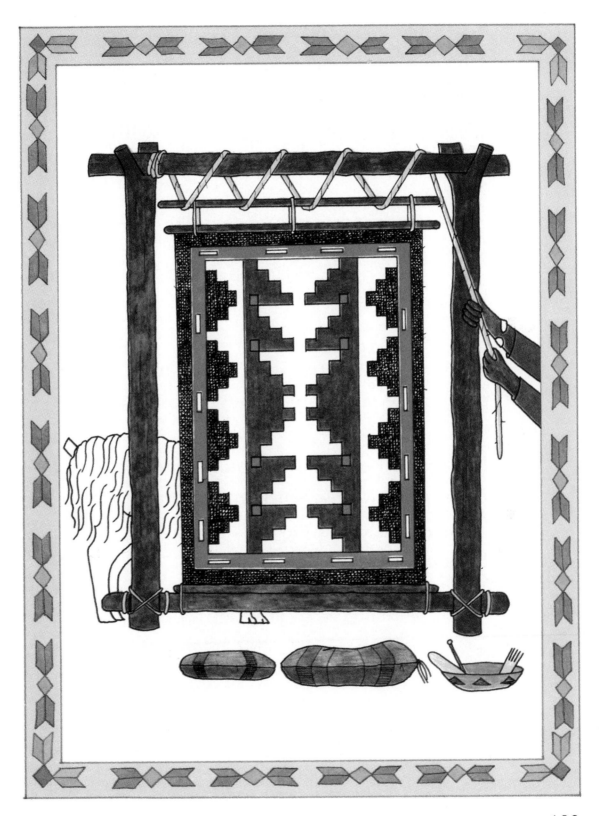

103

Since then, my wool has grown almost long enough for Glenmae and me to make another rug. I hope we do very soon. Because, you see, there aren't too many weavers like Glenmae left among the Navajos.

And there's only one goat like me, Geraldine.

Reader's Response ∽ What part of the story made you want to laugh most?

Library Link ∽ *If you would like to learn more about Native American life, read* Navajo: Herders, Weavers, and Silversmiths *by Sonia Bleeker.*

About
Window Rock

Here is a picture of Window Rock, the place described in the story. Do you see how the hole is like a window to the sky?

Window Rock is an important place for the Navajo people. Nearby is the Navajo Nation Museum where you can learn about the Navajos and their history. The Tribal Council meets nearby to make important decisions.

Every September the Navajo nation gathers at Window Rock for a big fair and rodeo games. Other Native American groups join in the fun.

Animals
That Migrate

from the book by Caroline Arnold

Some animals live in one place all the time.

A woodmouse, for example, never goes farther than 100 yards from the burrow in which it was born.

But some animals have two homes. Often these animals go long distances to get from one home to the other. We say that these animals migrate.

Most people know that many birds migrate. Ducks and other birds fly south every fall. You may see and hear them as they pass over where you live. In the spring they fly north again.

But many other kinds of animals migrate. Did you know that some insects migrate? Some fish migrate. Some reptiles and mammals migrate too. Even people sometimes migrate.

Why do animals migrate? There are many reasons. Sometimes they migrate because of the weather. Their summer home may be too cold in the winter, or their winter home may be too hot in the summer. Sometimes animals migrate when it is time for their babies to be born. They move to a place that is safe for the young animals. And sometimes animals migrate to find food.

Some animals go thousands of miles when they migrate. They may cross oceans or mountains. They may pass through terrible storms.

The Arctic Tern

An amazing trip is made each year by a bird called the arctic tern. During the summer arctic terns live near the north pole. There they build their nests and bring up their babies.

By August the weather begins to get cold. But when it is winter at the north pole, it will be summer at the south pole. So the arctic terns fly all the way to the south pole. That's about 11,000 miles away!

It takes them several months to make the trip. Then, after only a few months, summer is over at the south pole. It is time for these birds to return to the north pole! Each year the arctic tern flies about 22,000 miles!

The Chinook Salmon

The Chinook salmon lives on the Pacific coast of the United States. It is a fish that migrates. A young salmon hatches in a shallow stream. It lives in the stream for a few weeks. Then it begins to swim downstream.

Soon it leaves the stream where it was born. It swims into bigger and bigger rivers until at last it gets to the ocean. It is a dangerous trip. Dams, pollution, and bigger fish are all dangerous to young salmon.

Not all salmon reach the ocean. Those that do stay there for from two to five years. Then they return to the stream where they were born. Sometimes a salmon must swim 800 miles to get back to its stream!

How does it know the way? Each river and stream has its own smell. A salmon knows the smell of its own stream. It can smell its way back. The trip home is much harder than the trip to the ocean. This time the salmon must go upstream, against the way the water moves.

Salmon are strong. They have to be to make the trip. They can swim fast, and they can jump high into the air. Often they must jump over rocks and up waterfalls. Usually many salmon make the trip home at the same time.

At last they arrive. Then they mate. New salmon are born. The adult salmon die. In a few weeks the new salmon will begin their trip to the ocean.

The California Gray Whale

Many kinds of mammals migrate. Some mammals live on land. Others live in the sea.

California gray whales are mammals that live in the sea. They have their babies during January and February. The baby whales are born in warm water near California and Mexico. They drink milk and get fat. Later their fat will help keep them warm.

By March the babies are big enough to travel. Then all the whales start on a 6,000 mile trip. It will take them about three months. The whales are going to the Bering Sea.

Whales eat small plants called plankton. They also eat small sea animals called krill. These grow best in cold water. The Bering Sea is in the arctic. It is very cold. The whales will find plenty of food there.

All summer the whales eat and get fat. But when winter comes, they move south again. It is time for new babies to be born.

How do the whales find their way? Whales can hear very well. They listen to echoes in the water to find their way.

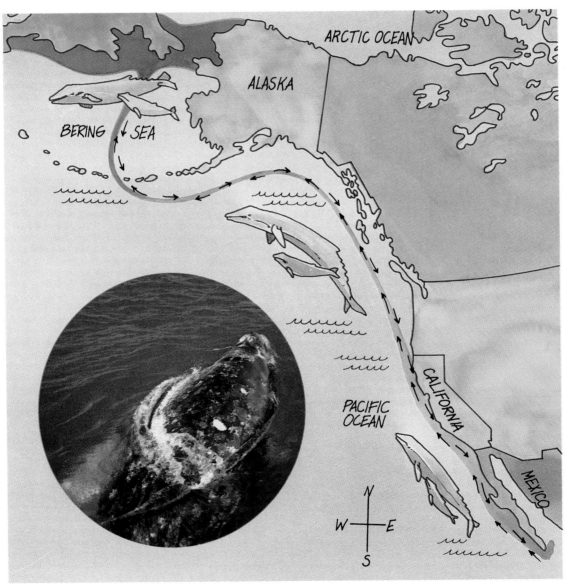

Many animals migrate. They make their homes in the same places as thousands of animals have before, and they follow the same paths to get there.

An animal is born knowing when and how to migrate. It uses its senses to find its way. Smell, taste, sight, touch, and hearing are all important.

Sometimes an animal migrates because of the weather. Sometimes it migrates to have babies. Sometimes it migrates to find food.

Sometimes one home does not have everything that an animal needs. An animal migrates because migration helps it to live.

Reader's Response ∽ Which animal makes the most difficult trip? Tell why you think so.

On the Move

In this article you found out that many animals don't spend the whole year in one place. Some people in the world spend a lot of time moving, too. They are called *nomads*. Many carry their homes with them.

The Bedouin are people who lived as nomads in the Middle East and northern Africa for many centuries. Some Bedouin still live as herders who take care of sheep and goats. They travel across the dry desert lands. Camels used to carry their tents. Today the herders sometimes use trucks.

A Salmon for Simon

written by Betty Waterton

illustrated by Ann Blades

All summer Simon had been fishing for salmon.

Last year, when he was little, his sisters had taught him how to catch minnows with a strainer. But this year his father had given him a fishing pole of his own, and he had been fishing for a salmon every day.

He hadn't caught a single salmon.

Now it was September. It was the time of year when many salmon were swimming past the island where Simon lived, near the west coast of Canada. They were returning from the sea, looking for the rivers and little streams where they had been born. There they would lay their eggs so that more salmon could be born.

114

One day, when the tide was on its way
out, Simon and his two sisters went clam-
digging. As soon as their pail was full of
clams, his sisters took them home to their
mother to cook for supper, but Simon stayed
at the beach. He had his fishing pole with
him, as he had every day that summer.

"I'm going to stay and fish for a
salmon," he thought. And he did.

He sat on a rock and fished.
He sat on a dock and fished.
But he didn't even see a salmon.

He stood on the edge of the beach
and fished.

He saw red and purple starfish sticking
to the rocks.

He saw small green crabs scuttling
among the seaweed.

He saw flat white sand dollars lying
on the wet sand.

He saw pink sea-anemones waving, pale
jellyfish floating, and shiners swimming.

But he didn't see a salmon.

"Is it ever hard to catch a salmon," thought Simon. He decided to stop fishing. Maybe forever.

Simon walked back along the beach to the place where he and his sisters had been clam-digging. The sea water had oozed up from the bottom of the hole and filled it. Three seagulls sat beside it. When Simon came near, they flew up into the air crying "Keer, keer, keer."

"I'm not good at catching salmon, but I am a good clam-digger," thought Simon.

He dug a few clams and put them on a nearby rock. The gulls flew down, picked up the clams in their beaks, carried them into the air and then dropped them. The clams hit the rocks and broke open.

Simon listened to the "bang, bang, pop" of the clam shells as they broke. He watched the gulls fly down and eat the soft clams.

Then Simon heard something different. Something sounding like FLAP, FLAP, FLAP.

119

"What's that?" he cried, but nobody answered.

He heard it again, FLAP, FLAP, FLAP, and this time it was right above his head.

The seagulls flew off, calling "Keer, keer, keer." Simon looked up—it was an eagle.

Its wings beat the air FLAP, FLAP, FLAP as it climbed towards the treetops. Simon had often seen bald eagles, but this one was different, for it was carrying something in its talons—something that glistened.

"A fish!" cried Simon, "he's got a FISH!"

He was so excited that he began hopping about and flapping his arms like eagles' wings. The seagulls were excited too, and they circled overhead, screeching.

In all the stir and confusion, the eagle dropped the fish. Down it came out of the sky,

down

down

down

down

down

SPLAAT.........SPLASH

into the clam hole!

120

The fish lay on its side in the shallow water and did not move.

Simon ran over to it. "It's dead," he cried.

Suddenly the fish flicked its tail and flipped over right side up. Its gills opened and closed and its fins began to move slowly.

"It's alive," shouted Simon. Then he looked closer. His eyes grew round. "It's alive and it's a SALMON," he cried. "It must be the most beautiful fish in the world," thought Simon.

For it was a coho, or silver salmon, which had come from far out in the Pacific Ocean to find the stream where it had been born. It had grown big in the ocean, and strong, and it shone like silver.

All summer Simon had been waiting to catch just such a fish, and here was one right in front of him. Yet he didn't feel happy.

He watched the big handsome fish pushing its nose against the gravelly sides of the clam hole, trying to find a way out, and he felt sorry for it. He knew it would die if it didn't have enough water to swim in. If only it could get back to the sea, it would live.

Simon wanted the salmon to be safe in the sea where it could swim and leap and dive. And where it would one day find its own stream. He didn't know how he was going to save the salmon. But he had to find a way.

"I won't let you die, Sukai," said Simon. (Sukai was an old Indian name for the salmon, and it meant "king of the fishes.")

Simon thought of carrying the fish to the sea, but he knew it was too big and heavy and too slippery for him to pick up.

He thought about waiting for the tide to come in, but he knew the salmon couldn't wait that long.

He looked up at the watching seagulls, but all they said was "Keer, keer."

He MUST find a way.

Looking around, he saw his clam shovel, and an idea popped into Simon's head.

He would dig a channel for the salmon to swim down to the sea. That was all he had to do. He began to dig and the wet sand was heavy, but he would do it!

He dug and dug.

After a while he stopped and looked to see how far he had gone, and he had not gone very far at all. He kept on digging.

His mother called him for supper but he couldn't go because he hadn't finished yet.

The salmon was lying quietly now in the shallow water, waiting.

The sun dipped low in the sky and the air became cool. Simon's hands were red and he was getting a blister, but he kept on digging.

At last, just when he thought he couldn't lift another shovelful of sand, he looked up and there he was, at the pool.

The channel was finished.

Cold sea water flowed into it. When the salmon felt the freshness of the sea, it began to move again. Its nose found the opening to the channel and slowly, slowly the salmon began to swim down it.

Down to the sea.

Simon watched his shining salmon. Down, down, down the channel it swam. At last it reached the sea.

It dived deep into the cool green water, and then, gleaming in the last rays of the setting sun, it gave a great leap into the air.

And it seemed to Simon that the salmon flicked its tail as if to say "thank you" before it disappeared beneath the waves.

"Good-bye, Sukai," called Simon.

The salmon was free at last.

Soon it would be in the deep, secret places of the sea.

Now the sun had set and a chilly wind was starting to blow. Simon's hands were sore and his feet were cold, but he felt warm inside. And happy. He picked up his fishing pole and his shovel and started for home.

And he knew, as he got near his house, that it would be bright and cheery inside because lamplight shone golden through the windows.

And he knew that it would be nice and warm, because he could see smoke curling out of the chimney.

And he knew that something good was cooking for supper because he could smell a delicious smell.

And Simon thought, as he opened the door, that maybe he would go fishing again tomorrow, after all.

But not for a salmon.

Reader's Response ∼ What would you do if you found an animal that needed help?

A Tale From Simon's Home

Native North Americans have many tales about the eagle. In her book *Totem Pole*, Diane Hoyt-Goldsmith tells of an eagle that lives near a fishing village much like Simon's home.

One day a young chief finds a magnificent eagle trapped in an old fishing net. The chief untangles the bird and then sets it free.

Many months later, the people in the chief's village cannot find food. As the worried chief walks on the beach, a beautiful salmon drops at his feet. Looking up, the chief sees the eagle flying away.

From then on, the tale says, the eagle leaves food every day. It repays the young chief's kindness many, many times.

FEATHERS LIKE A RAINBOW

An Amazon Indian Tale

story and pictures by Flora

A long, long time ago, the birds of the great rain forest around the Amazon River had dark feathers.

"Why are our feathers so ugly?" Jacamin, a gray-winged trumpeter, asked his mother. "Why can't I have feathers as beautiful as the rainbow? Why can't I have feathers as bright as the flowers and butterflies we see around us?"

"I will try to find the colors for you, my son," his mother promised.

As Jacamin's mother walked through the
forest, she met Macaw.

"Hello, my friend," she said. "Do you know
where I can find colors as beautiful as the rainbow
and as bright as the flowers and butterflies of the
rain forest? I want them for my son's feathers."

"No," replied Macaw, "but I too would like some color in my feathers. Let us search together."

As the two birds walked deeper and deeper into the forest, they met many other birds. They all wanted bright colors for their feathers.

But they looked in vain.

By the end of the day, the birds were tired and discouraged. "We'll never find the colors," said Macaw.

Suddenly something bright and brilliant darted by.

"What was that?" cried Toucan.

"It can't be a firefly, fireflies only shine in the dark of the night," said Macaw.

"It flew too quickly to be a butterfly," said Ibis.

"It was too close to be a star," said Woodpecker.

"Look! It is a tiny bird!" cried Cock-of-the-rock.

The tiny bird was covered with feathers so bright the birds had to blink their eyes. They watched it hover in the air and flit from flower to flower.

"What is your name, and where did you get your beautiful feathers?" Jacamin's mother asked.

"I am Hummingbird, and I get my beautiful feathers from the flowers," said the bird. "Every day I kiss the flowers of the rain forest. From each I take a dab of color and drop it into my bowl. Then I splash a little of each color on my feathers."

The other birds could hardly
wait for the next day. They all
wanted to copy Hummingbird!
As soon as the sun rose, they rushed
to the flowers. But most of the birds
were too heavy to hover in the air,
and their beaks were too big
to reach inside the flowers the way
Hummingbird's did.

"It's useless," said Macaw sadly.

Jacamin's mother was saddest
of all. She had promised to find the
colors for her son. Then, suddenly,
she had an idea. She would steal the
bowl of colors from Hummingbird!

She grabbed the bowl and
hurried home.

"Here, my son," she said. "I have brought you Hummingbird's colors. Go quickly and wash yourself in the bowl before the other birds see you."

But it was too late!

The birds swooped down on Jacamin and
snatched away the bowl. Then they bathed
themselves in Hummingbird's colors. Macaw took
red, orange, green, and blue. Woodpecker took red
and blue. Toucan took green, yellow, and red, and
Ibis pink. Cock-of-the-rock took bright orange.

Jacamin stood by sadly, watching the brightly colored birds fly joyously among the trees.

"Where are your colors?" asked his mother.

"The birds stole them from me," Jacamin said.

"Well, go and get them back, silly boy," said his mother. She was so angry she threw ashes on his back.

When Jacamin got to Hummingbird's bowl, there was only a dot of purple left. He rubbed it on his breast.

To this very day the gray-winged trumpeter has a purple breast and an ash-gray back.

As for the other birds of the Amazon, they too still wear the colors stolen from Hummingbird so long ago.

Only the hummingbird has *all* the colors. His feathers are as beautiful as the rainbow, and as bright as the flowers and butterflies of the great rain forest around the Amazon River.

Reader's Response ∽ Did you like this way of explaining how the birds got their colors? Can you think of another way?

GLOSSARY

Full pronunciation key* The pronunciation of each word is shown just after the word, in this way: **abbreviate** (ə brē'vē āt).

The letters and signs used are pronounced as in the words below.

The mark ' is placed after a syllable with primary or heavy accent as in the example above.

The mark ' after a syllable shows a secondary or lighter accent, as in **abbreviation** (ə brē'vē ā'shən).

SYMBOL	KEY WORDS	SYMBOL	KEY WORDS	SYMBOL	KEY WORDS
a	ask, fat	u	up, cut	r	red, dear
ā	ape, date	ʉr	fur, fern	s	sell, pass
ä	car, father			t	top, hat
		ə	**a** in ago	v	vat, have
e	elf, ten		**e** in agent	w	will, always
er	berry, care		**e** in father	y	yet, yard
ē	even, meet		**i** in unity	z	zebra, haze
			o in collect		
i	is, hit		**u** in focus	ch	chin, arch
ir	mirror, here			ñg	ring, singer
ī	ice, fire	b	bed, dub	sh	she, dash
		d	did, had	th	thin, truth
o	lot, pond	f	fall, off	*th*	then, father
ō	open, go	g	get, dog	zh	s in pleasure
ô	law, horn	h	he, ahead		
oi	oil, point	j	joy, jump	'	as in (ā'b'l)
ᴏᴏ	look, pull	k	kill, bake		
o͞o	ooze, tool	l	let, ball		
yᴏᴏ	unite, cure	m	met, trim		
yo͞o	cute, few	n	not, ton		
ou	out, crowd	p	put, tap		

*Pronunciation key and respellings adapted from *Webster's New World Dictionary, Basic School Edition,*

144

A

a·dult (ə dult′ *or* ad′ult) **1.** fully grown: "*Adult* whales travel six thousand miles with their baby whales." **2.** a grown-up person or animal.

am·bu·lance (am′byə ləns) a car or wagon used to carry sick or hurt people: "The *ambulance* raced to the hospital."

arc·tic (ärk′tik *or* är′tik) **1.** near the North Pole: "The *arctic* air is very cold." **2.** the land, water, and air around or close to the North Pole.

axe (aks) a tool for chopping wood: "She swung the *axe* into the log."

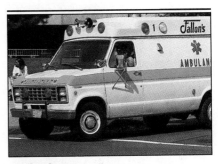

ambulance

B

belief (bə lēf′) an idea or a feeling that certain things are true: "Many people have the *belief* that ostriches stick their heads in the sand when they are frightened."

blis·ter (blis′tər) small swollen place on the skin filled with water caused by a burn or rubbing: "He got a *blister* on his hand after batting the ball."

breathe (brē*th*) take air into the lungs and then let it out: "The doctor asked me to *breathe* deeply."

bump (bump) **1.** knock against something. **2.** a part that sticks out: "Her bike shook when she rode over the *bump*."

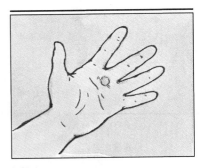

blister

C

cartwheel

chimney

clam-digging

care·ful·ly (ker′fəl lē) gently, with attention so as not to have mistakes or accidents: "Cross the street *carefully.*"

car·rot (kar′ət) a plant with a long, thick orange-red root that is eaten as a vegetable: "I ate a *carrot* with my lunch."

cart·wheel (kärt′hwēl) a handspring done sideways: "Do your *cartwheel* on the mat."

cat·a·log (kat″l ôg *or* kat″l og) **1.** a book listing things for sale. **2.** having to do with such a book: "We went to the *catalog* store to get the doll."

ce·ment (si ment′) **1.** to fasten together with a mixture of clay, limestone, and water or with any soft substance that makes things stick to each other when it hardens: "Tom will *cement* the pieces of the dish he broke." **2.** a paste or glue.

chan·nel (chan″l) a body of water joining two larger bodies of water: "The salmon swam through the *channel* and then out to the sea."

chim·ney (chim′nē) a pipe going through a roof to carry away smoke from a fireplace or furnace: "A fireplace *chimney* often has brick around it."

clam-dig·ging (klam′ dig′ing) turning up sand or mud with a shovel or rake to look for clams: "Yesterday the whole family went *clam-digging,* so that we could eat clams for dinner."

col·lec·tion (kə lek′shən) a group of things gathered together that belong together: "Nora is proud of her baseball card *collection.*"

combs (kōmz) **1.** thin strips of metal or plastic with teeth used to arrange a person's hair. **2.** tools with metal teeth for cleaning and straightening wool: "She cleaned the sheep's hair with the *combs.*"

com·mon (kom'ən) usual: "Birds are *common* in the woods."

con·fus·ion (kən fyōō'zhən) a state of disorder: "There was *confusion* in the air when three sea gulls dove for the same clam."

cur·tains (kʉr't'nz) cloth hung on windows and doors: "We opened the *curtains* to let in the bright light."

a fat	ȯi oil	ch chin
ā ape	oo look	sh she
ä car, father	ōō tool	th thin
e ten	ou out	*th* then
er care	u up	zh leisure
ē even	ur fur	n̂g ring
i hit		
ir here	ə = a *in* ago	
ī bite, fire	e *in* agent	
o lot	i *in* unity	
ō go	o *in* collect	
ô law, horn	u *in* focus	

D

dan·ger·ous (dān'jər əs) not safe: "It is *dangerous* to cross the street without looking both ways."

dif·fi·cult (dif'i kəlt) hard to do: "It is *difficult* to put these boots on."

dye (dī) something used to color cloth, hair, or other materials: "She dipped the shirt in dark blue *dye*."

curtains

E

ea·gle (ē'g'l) a large, strong bird with excellent eyesight that captures and eats other birds and animals: "The *eagle* flew high above the water."

ech·oes (ek'ōz) sounds heard again when the sound waves bounce back off a surface: "We heard our *echoes* as we called to each other inside the tunnel."

en·e·my (en'ə mē) a person, group, or animal that is not a friend: "A cat is a mouse's *enemy*."

dye

F

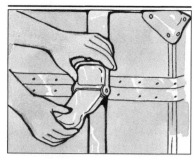

fastened

fa·ble (fa′b′l) **1.** a very short story that teaches a lesson. **2.** a story or belief that is not true: "The belief that bats are blind is a *fable*."

fact (fakt) something that really happened or is true: "It is a *fact* that cats are animals."

fas·tened (fas″nd) made something stay in place or attached two things together: "Howard *fastened* the lid on the trunk."

fi·bers (fī′bərz) threads or very thin hair-like parts of an animal or plant: "The cotton *fibers* were thinner than hairs."

fid·dle·sticks (fid″l stiks′) nonsense: "*Fiddlesticks!* I can't do that!"

flicked (flikt) gave a light, quick stroke to something: "I *flicked* the bug off the plant."

foil (foil) metal made into very thin sheets, as in aluminum foil: "The meat was wrapped in *foil* to keep in the juices."

fibers

G

garage

ga·rage (gə rozh′ *or* gə räj′) a place for keeping cars: "Park the car in the *garage*."

gi·gan·tic (jī gan′tik) huge, like a giant; very big; very large; enormous: "The elephant looked *gigantic* to the little boy."

gleam·ing (glēm′ing) with a shining surface: "The sea was *gleaming* in the sunlight."

glis·tened (glis″nd) shone or sparkled: "The salmon *glistened* in the sunlight."

grav·el·ly (grav″l ē) made from small stones and pebbles: "The *gravelly* road was very bumpy."

greet·ings (grēt′iĝs) a friendly wish to someone: "José sent holiday *greetings* to his grandfather."

a fat	**oi** oil	**ch** chin
ā ape	**oo** look	**sh** she
ä car, father	**o͞o** tool	**th** thin
e ten	**ou** out	***th*** then
er care	**u** up	**zh** leisure
ē even	**ur** fur	**n̂g** ring
i hit		
ir here	**ə** = a *in* ago	
ī bite, fire	e *in* agent	
o lot	i *in* unity	
ō go	o *in* collect	
ô law, horn	u *in* focus	

H

Hal·low·een (hal′ə wēn′) the evening of October 31, celebrated by children in costumes asking for treats: "I'm making a costume to wear on *Halloween*."

ham·mer·ing (ham′ər iĝ) hitting many times with a hammer or hard object: "She liked *hammering* the nails into the tree house."

har·mon·i·ca (här mon′ i kə) a small musical instrument played by blowing air into it: "I played a tune on my *harmonica*."

hos·pi·tal (hos′pi t′l) a place for the care of the sick or injured: "Doctor Lo works at the *hospital*."

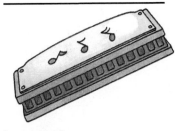

harmonica

I

in·sects (in′sekts) small animals with six legs and usually two pairs of wings: "Flies and ants are examples of *insects*."

K

knot (not) tight loop in a rope or string: "Gloria tied a *knot* in the rope."

krill

krill (kril) very small sea animals like tiny shrimp that some whales eat: "Whales' mouths have small holes that let water out but trap *krill*."

L

laun·dro·mat (lôn'drə mat) a place where a person pays to use a washing machine and a clothes dryer: "Tom took the clothes to the *laundromat*."

laun·dry bag (lôn'drē bag') a sack, often made of cloth, used to carry clothes to be washed: "Mary kept her dirty clothes in a *laundry bag*."

loom (lo͞om) a frame upon which yarn is stretched for weaving: "He started to work at the *loom*."

loom

M

mag·ni·fied (mag'nə fīd) made something look larger than it really is: "The lens *magnified* the size of the insect."

mam·mals (mam'əlz) animals that feed their young with milk from the mother: "People, cows, and whales are examples of *mammals*."

mead·ow (med'ō) a level, grassy piece of land: "Tony fell asleep in the *meadow*."

mi·grate (mī'grāt) move from one place to another: "Many birds *migrate* to warmer places in winter."

mix·ture (miks'chər) something made by combining different things: "Mud is a *mixture* of dirt and water."

mo·hair (mō'her) the silky hair of an angora goat, which is spun into yarn: "She wore a sweater made of *mohair*."

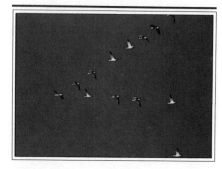

migrate

mus·tache (mə stash′ *or* mus′tash) **1.** the hair that a man lets grow out above his upper lip: "The barber trimmed the man's *mustache*." **2.** the hair or bristles around an animal's mouth.

a fat	oi oil	ch chin	
ā ape	oo look	sh she	
ä car, father	o͞o tool	th thin	
e ten	ou out	th then	
er care	u up	zh leisure	
ē even	ur fur	n̂g ring	
i hit			
ir here	ə = a *in* ago		
ī bite, fire	e *in* agent		
o lot	i *in* unity		
ō go	o *in* collect		
ô law, horn	u *in* focus		

N

neigh·bor (nā′bər) someone who lives in the next house or nearby: "Joe is our nearest *neighbor*."

news·pa·per (no͞oz′pā′pər *or* nyo͞oz′pā′pər) sheets of paper printed each day that tell the news and other information: "Mother reads the *newspaper* every morning."

O

os·trich·es (ôs′trich iz) large birds with long necks and legs: "*Ostriches* cannot fly."

neighbor

P

pack·age (pak′ij) things wrapped up, usually in paper or in a box: "Susan put the cookies in a *package* and mailed it to her aunt."

pat·tern (pat′ərn) **1.** a plan used as a guide to make something. **2.** a design, that often repeats: "We repeated the *pattern*: stars, squares—stars, squares on the shirt we decorated."

peb·bles (peb″lz) tiny stones worn smooth: "Roberto liked to search for shiny, white *pebbles*."

ostriches

plankton

pen·cils (pen's'lz) thin rods of soft materials, such as graphite or wax, enclosed in wood or metal and used for writing or drawing: "Miya used her new *pencils* to write in her notebook."

plank·ton (plañgk'tən) tiny plants and animals floating in water: "Some fish eat *plankton*."

plas·tic (plas'tik) a material made from oil or other chemicals that can be hardened into useful things: "Amanda's whistle was made from *plastic*."

pol·lu·tion (pə loo'shən) dirt or harmful substances in the air, water, or ground: "Cars add to the air *pollution* in our city."

por·cu·pines (pôr'kyoo pīnz) animals covered with sharp spines or quills: "*Porcupines* use their quills to protect themselves."

prac·tice (prak'tis) the doing of something again and again to learn to do it well: "Piano *practice* makes my playing better."

prob·a·bly (prob'ə blē) more likely than not: "It will *probably* rain tomorrow."

porcupines

Q

quills (kwilz) **1.** pens made from feathers. **2.** stiff, sharp hairs that stick out of a porcupine's body: "The tips of the porcupine's *quills* are sharp."

R

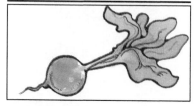

radish

rad·ish (rad'ish) a small, crisp root with red or white skin: "A *radish* can be eaten in a salad."

rep·tiles (rep't'lz *or* rep'tīlz) coldblooded animals that crawl on their bellies or creep on short legs: "Turtles, snakes, and lizards are *reptiles*."

S

a fat	**oi** oil	**ch** chin
ā ape	**oo** look	**sh** she
ä car, father	**ōo** tool	**th** thin
e ten	**ou** out	**th** then
er care	**u** up	**zh** leisure
ē even	**ur** fur	**ng** ring
i hit		
ir here	ə = a *in* ago	
ī bite, fire	e *in* agent	
o lot	i *in* unity	
ō go	o *in* collect	
ô law, horn	u *in* focus	

salm·on (sam'ən) large fish with silver scales and reddish meat that is eaten for food: "*Salmon* swim upriver to lay their eggs."

scis·sors (siz'ərz) a tool for cutting: "These *scissors* are sharp."

screech·ing (skrēch'ing) making a harsh, shrill sound: "We could hear the gulls *screeching* as we walked to the beach."

scut·tling (skut"ling) hurrying quickly: "Tiny tadpoles were *scuttling* about the weeds."

sea-a·nem·o·ne or **sea a·nem·o·ne** (sē'ə nem'ə nē) a sea animal often brightly colored that looks like a flower: "The *sea-anemone* gently floated in the water."

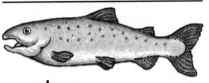

salmon

sea·gull or **sea gull** (sē'gul) a large sea bird with large wings, webbed feet, and gray and white feathers: "The *seagull* flew over the beach looking for food."

sharp·en·ing (shär'p'n ing) making sharp or pointed: "She is *sharpening* the pencil."

skip·per (skip'ər) **1.** the captain of a ship. **2.** a kind of fish that can skip or hop on its fins and belly: "A *skipper* can hop over the muddy shore."

smeared (smird) to rub or spread on: "He *smeared* mud on his foot."

soc·cer (sok'ər) a ball game played between two teams in which the ball is kicked, but not touched by the hands of the players: "Kelly is on the school *soccer* team."

talons

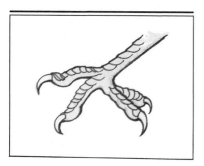

tern

travel

spin·dle (spin′d′l) a thin rod used to twist and hold thread in spinning: "Spin the thread around and around the *spindle*."

sprin·kler (spriñg′klər) a device for scattering water: "The children cooled off under the *sprinkler* in the back yard."

squawked (skwôkt) made a loud, harsh sound: "The hen *squawked* because she was scared."

suit·case (so͞ot′kās) a bag used for carrying clothes when traveling: "We each packed our own *suitcase* for the trip."

T

tal·ons (tal′ənz) the claws of a bird that kills other animals for food: "The eagle grabbed onto the mouse with its *talons*."

tern (tʉrn) a sea bird: "A *tern* has a thin body, a long beak, and a fork-shaped tail."

thor·ough·ly (thʉr′ō lē) very completely: "We searched the grass *thoroughly* for the lost ring."

trav·el (trav″l) go from one place to another: "We like to *travel* by airplane."

V

veg·e·ta·ble gar·den (vej′tə b′l *or* vej′ə tə b′l gär′d′n) a piece of land where plants are grown for food: "We grow carrots, corn, and beans in our *vegetable garden*."

W

war·ri·or (wôr′ē ər) a soldier: "He dreamed of being a brave and famous *warrior.*"

weave (wēv) make cloth by putting threads over and under one another: "People *weave* thread into cloth."

wool (wo͝ol) **1.** soft curly hair of sheep or the hair of goats or llamas: "A sheep's *wool* is nice to touch." **2.** yarn or cloth made from this hair.

wrapped (rapt) wound or folded something around an object: "He *wrapped* the string around and around his finger."

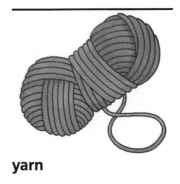

yarn

Y

yarn (yärn) thread that is spun for use in weaving or knitting: "I bought red *yarn* to make the hat."

yes·ter·day (yes′tər dē *or* yes′tər dā) the day before today: "I had my hair cut *yesterday.*"

young (yun͡g) not old: "The *young* tree stood only two feet tall."

yuc·ca (yuk′ə) a tall plant with long, pointed leaves and white flowers on a long stem: "She used the roots of the *yucca* plant to make soapy suds."

yucca

155

ABOUT THE
Authors & Illustrators

ALAN ARKIN

✳ Alan Arkin was born in New York City. He has
written three books for young people. They are
Tony's Hard Work Day, The Lemming Condition, and
Clearing. Tony's Hard Work Day is a story based on
his own family when his children were young. Alan
Arkin is also an actor, a movie director, and a
songwriter. He began his entertainment career as a
folk singer. *(Born 1934)*

JOSE ARUEGO

■ Jose Aruego was born in the Philippines. His
family did not want him to become an artist. But he
chose to pursue a boyhood dream of illustrating. As
a child he collected comic books. He began his
artistic career by drawing cartoons like the ones he
admired in the comics. Later he switched to
illustrating children's books. Jose Aruego likes to
draw animals doing funny antics in his books. He
has won numerous awards for his illustrations. He
and his wife, Ariane Dewey, worked together
illustrating *Mitchell Is Moving. (Born 1932)*

156

ANN BLADES

■ Ann Blades first decided to make books for children when she was a teacher. She taught at Mile 18, a small farming community in British Columbia. Ann Blades noticed that there were no books about children that lived lives like her own students, so she decided to write and paint one. In fact, she used one of the children in her class as a model for the pictures. Her first book, *Mary of Mile 18*, is about a girl who wants to adopt a wolf puppy. Her illustrations in *A Salmon for Simon* won the Canadian Library Association's Amelia Frances Howard-Gibbon Illustrator's Award and the Canada Council Children's Award. *(Born 1947)*

FLORA

▲ Flora Castaño Ferreira's interest in the beauty of the rain forest grew from her love of her grandfather's work. He was a naturalist in Brazil. The first word she said as a tiny child was "beautiful." She uses vivid colors to portray the birds, butterflies, and flowers in the rain forest. *Feathers Like a Rainbow* is her first book. Flora Castaño Ferreira lives in New York City, but she likes to visit her grandchildren in South America. *(Born 1917)*

157

MARJORIE WEINMAN SHARMAT

✳ Marjorie Weinman Sharmat says, "My earliest ambition was to become a writer or a detective or a lion tamer. I began writing when I was eight." The hero of her book *Mitchell Is Moving* is her husband who also writes children's books. When she asked him what creature he would like to be, he replied, "a dinosaur," because he knew it liked slimy moss and mud. Marjorie Weinman Sharmat often bases her writing on real-life people and experiences. *(Born 1928)*

SALLY WITTMAN

■ Sally Wittman was born in Portland, Oregon. Her mother was a painter. Her father was a businessman. Sally Wittman says she had a lovely childhood. In her books, she writes about her own childhood experiences. She also writes about her own children and their friends. One of her books, *A Special Trade*, was an American Library Association Notable Book selection. *(Born 1941)*

158

Author Index

Grateful acknowledgment is made to the following publishers, authors, and agents for their permission to reprint copyrighted material. Every effort has been made to locate all copyright proprietors; any errors or omissions in copyright notice are inadvertent and will be corrected in future printings as they are discovered.

"Animal Fact/Animal Fable" excerpt from *Animal Fact/Animal Fable* by Seymour Simon, illustrated by Diane de Groat. Text copyright © 1979 by Seymour Simon. Illustrations copyright © 1979 by Diane de Groat. Reprinted by permission of Crown Publishers, Inc.

"Animals That Migrate" excerpt from *Animals That Migrate* by Caroline Arnold. Copyright © 1982 by Carolrhoda Books, Inc. Reprinted by permission of Carolrhoda Books, 241 First Avenue North, Minneapolis, MN 55401.

Feathers Like a Rainbow: An Amazon Indian Tale, written and illustrated by Flora, copyright © 1989 by Flora Castaño Ferreira. Reprinted by permission of HarperCollins Publishers.

"Gloria Who Might Be My Best Friend" from *The Stories Julian Tells* by Ann Cameron. Reprinted by permission of Pantheon Books, a Division of Random House, Inc., and of the British publisher, Victor Gollancz Ltd. Copyright © 1981 by Ann Cameron.

The Goat in the Rug by Charles L. Blood and Martin A. Link, illustrated by Nancy Winslow Parker. Reprinted by permission of Four Winds Press, an imprint of Macmillan Publishing Company. Text copyright © 1980 by Charles L. Blood and Martin A. Link. Illustrations copyright © 1980 by Nancy Winslow Parker.

Mitchell Is Moving by Marjorie Weinman Sharmat, illustrated by Jose Aruego and Ariane Dewey. Reprinted by permission of Macmillan Publishing Company, an imprint of Macmillan, Inc. Text copyright © 1978 by Marjorie Weinman Sharmat. Illustrations copyright © 1978 by Jose Aruego & Ariane Dewey.

"A Moment in Summer" from *River Winding* by Charlotte Zolotow. Text copyright © 1970 by Charlotte Zolotow. Reprinted by permission of HarperCollins Publishers.

"Reply to Someone Who Asked Why the Two of Us Are Such Good Friends" reprinted with permission of Atheneum Publishers, an imprint of Macmillan Publishing Company, and of the author's agent, Marian Reiner, from *A Week in the Life of Best Friends* by Beatrice Schenk de Regniers. Copyright © 1986 Beatrice Schenk de Regniers.

A Salmon for Simon by Betty Waterton, illustrated by Ann Blades. Text © 1978 by Betty Waterton. Illustrations © 1978 by Ann Blades. Reprinted by permission of Groundwood/Douglas & McIntyre Children's Books.

"Snail" by Langston Hughes. Copyright 1947 by Langston Hughes. Reprinted from *Selected Poems of Langston Hughes* by permission of Alfred A. Knopf, Inc., a Division of Random House, Inc.

A Special Trade by Sally Wittman. Illustrations by Karen Gundersheimer. Text copyright © 1978 by Sally Christensen Wittman. Illustrations © 1978 by Karen Gundersheimer. Reprinted by persmission of HarperCollins Publishers.

Tikki Tikki Tembo retold by Arlene Mosel, illustrated by Blair Lent. Text copyright © 1968 by Arlene Mosel, illustrations copyright © 1968 by Blair Lent, Jr. Reprinted by permission of Henry Holt and Company.

Tony's Hard Work Day by Alan Arkin. Pictures by James Stevenson. Text copyright © 1972 by Alan Arkin. Pictures copyright © 1972 by James Stevenson. Reprinted by permission of the author's agent, Matthew Arkin, and of the artist's agent, Liz Darhansoff.

COVER ILLUSTRATION: Lily Toy Hong

ILLUSTRATION: 1-7, Tamar Habar-Schaim; 12-26, Jose Aruego and Ariane Dewey; 27, Polo Barrera; 28-39, James Ransome; 40-41, Laura Tarrish; 42-54, James Stevenson; 55, Sucie Stevenson; 56-62, Karen Gundersheimer; 63, Robin Oz; 64-75 Blair Lent; 80-81, Steve Schindler; 82-90, Diane de Groat; 92-93, Bart Forbes; 94-104, Nancy Winslow Parker; 105, Polo Barrera; 114-130, Ann Blades; 131, Arieh Zeldich; 132-143, Flora Castaño Ferreira, border art Polo Barrera; 145, Eulala Connor; 146, Diane Dawson Hearn, Claudia Sargent, Eulala Connor; 147, Melinda Fabian, Roberta Holmes; 148, Eulala Connor, Claudia Sargent; 149, Deirdre Griffin; 150, Eulala Connor; 151, Deirdre Griffin; 152, Eulala Connor; 153, Susan David; 154, Eulala Connor, Diane Dawson Hearn; 155, Deirdre Griffin, Eulala Connor; 156-158, Tamar Haber-Schaim.

PHOTOGRAPHY: 8-9, Jo Browne/ Mick SMEE/TSW, Chicago; 9, THE FOURTH OF JULY, wool, cotton, and nylon fabrics hooked on a burlap ground, 37 1/2" x 45 1/2". American, ca. 1940. Gift of Mr. Fred MacMurray. Courtesy of the Shelburne Museum, Shelburne, Vermont; 76-77, Stephen Frink/The Stock Market; 77, CHESHIRE CAT IN CROUCHED POSITION, illustration by Randolph Caldecott, British, (1846-1886); 78, Ken O'Donoghue; 91, Photograph of Jane Goodall on page 10 from "The Chimpanzee Family Book", © 1989, Neugebauer Press, Salzburg, and used by arrangement with Picture Book Studio, Ltd. All rights reserved; 105, Jerry Jacka Photography; 106, Hans Reinhard/Bruce Coleman; 107, John Shaw/Bruce Coleman; 108, Gary Meczaros/Bruce Coleman; 111, Jeff Foott/Bruce Coleman; 112, Dotte Larson/Bruce Coleman; 113, Ed Lallo/Third Coast Stock Source; 145, Tom Pantages; 150, (t) Frank Siteman, (m) Jen & Des Bartlett/Bruce Coleman; 151, Suzanne Brookens/The Stock Market; 152, John Ebeling/Bruce Coleman; 154, Stephen G. Maka; 156, (t) Reuters/Bettmann Newsphotos, (b) courtesy Macmillan Publishing Co.; 157, (b) provided by the author; 157, (t) provided by the author; 158, (t) courtesy, Andrew Sharmat, (b) Harper & Row, Publishers, Inc.

160